An AMA Research Study

Performance Appraisal
A Study of Current Techniques

Evelyn Eichel
Henry E. Bender

Research and Information Service
American Management Associations

The authors would like to express their appreciation to Dr. John W. Enell for his contributions to the content and structure of this research report.

Library of Congress Cataloging in Publication Data

Eichel, Evelyn, 1956-
  Performance appraisal.

  Includes bibliographical references.
  1. Employees, Rating of.   I. Bender, Henry E.,
1938-   II. Title.
HF5549.5.R3E38   1984   658.3′125   84-451
ISBN 0-8144-3509-2

©1984 AMA Research and Information Service
American Management Associations, New York.
All rights reserved. Printed in the United States of America.

This management research study has been distributed to all members enrolled in the Human Resources Division of the American Management Associations. A limited supply of extra copies is available at $10.00 a copy for AMA members, $13.50 for non-members.

This publication may not be produced, stored in a retrieval system, or transmitted in whole or in part, in any form or by any means, electronic, mechanical, photographic, recorded, or otherwise, without prior written permission of AMA Research and Information Service, 135 West 50th Street, New York, N.Y. 10020.

First Printing

Contents

About This Study — 5
Summary — 7
1. Performance Appraisal: An Overview — 9
    Appraisal Defined — 9
        Research Methods — 10
    Evolving Purposes of Appraisal — 11
    A Function of Human Resources — 13
    Who Participates — 13
        Who is Appraised — 13
        Who Does the Appraising — 15
    The Performance Appraisal Process — 17
        Goal Setting — 17
        Job Analysis — 18
        Job Descriptions — 20
        Performance Standards and Appraisal — 20
    Problem Areas — 21
        Adverse Effects on Multiple Uses — 22
        Unexpected Requirements — 25
        Legal Context — 26
2. Performance Appraisal Techniques — 32
    Comparative Methods — 34
        Ranking — 34
        Paired Comparisons — 35
        Forced Distribution — 35
        Pros and Cons of
            Comparative Methods — 35
    Absolute Methods — 37
        The Essay Approach — 37
        Weighted Checklists — 38
        Critical Incidents — 39
        Graphic Rating Scales — 41
        Behaviorally Anchored Rating Scales — 43
    Outcome-Oriented Techniques — 43
        The Direct Index — 45
        Standards of Performance — 47
        Management by Objectives — 48

Comparison of Appraisal Techniques	51
Purposes and Techniques	53
The Feedback Interview	55
Are Performance Appraisals Worthwhile?	57
Appendix	58
References	60

About This Study

MANY management theorists hold that performance appraisal is one of the most important management processes. Most management practitioners agree that appraisal is an important component of their jobs, but point out that it is a difficult one to carry out. Employees often complain that appraisals are not made with objectivity and fairness. Performance appraisals are widely used in connection with decisions in the sensitive area of pay increases. Dissatisfaction with increases can lead to criticism of the appraisal process, and to claims of distortion of the appraisal for reasons of favoritism or company politics.

In the past decade, concern for equal opportunity in the workplace has directed still more attention to the appraisal process. Recognizing that selection criteria and performance appraisal are critical elements in the equitable treatment of minority groups and women in the employment world, federal regulations have been extended to these areas.

Good methods of performance appraisal—when well carried out in practice—can motivate employees by providing evenhanded recognition of their efforts, can help with mapping out career paths, can give guidance as to needed training and development, and can reduce the risk of governmental legal challenges based on EEOC standards and regulations.

The goals are worthwhile, but there are a number of routes to them, and reports from the field suggest that there are some serious potholes, broken water mains and even detours along the way. This makes it seem advisable to re-examine company experiences with alternative forms of performance appraisal from time to time in a search for better directions.

Arthur Meidan gave a helpful review of performance appraisal methods in his report in the AMA Management Briefing series in 1981. Entitled "The Appraisal of Managerial Performance," this provides important insights into methods and procedures for evaluation of managerial performance. Donald L. Kirkpatrick added valuable concepts and outstanding case material in his AMACOM book, "How to Improve Performance Through Appraisal and Coaching" (1982).

The present research study used a survey of management personnel to add new data on performance appraisal practices in the field and on thinking among practitioners. The report which follows records current practice. It goes well beyond statistical summaries, however. It adds and compares findings from an extensive literature review and from interviews with individuals with responsibilities for performance appraisals.

Dr. Evelyn Eichel is manager, management development at PepsiCo in Purchase, New York. She is familiar with appraisal methods being used by major business organizations and management consulting firms. She has been engaged in the study of performance appraisal methods for several years, and is concerned with the integration of the appraisal process into the total human resource function. She earned her B.A. degree from the State University of New York at Stonybrook, an M.A. from Hofstra University, and a Ph.D. in evaluation and applied psychology from Hofstra University.

Dr. Henry E. Bender joined the AMA staff as research director in 1977. He is also a principal consultant for Concept Applications, Ltd. His work has focused on organizational development and training, survey/marketing research, and man/systems interactions. He has assisted several organizations in the development of their performance appraisal systems. Dr. Bender earned Bachelor's and Master's degrees in psychology from Hofstra University, and his Ph.D. in the social sciences from New York University.

The authors would like to express their thanks to H. Tad Troutman, who gave invaluable aid with the analysis and presentation of data.

John W. Enell
Vice-President for Research (Ret.)

Henry E. Bender
Director of Research

Summary

PERFORMANCE appraisal is recognized as an important element of the jobs of managers and supervisors. It can provide significant help in meeting departmental and company objectives. It is valuable in the development of subordinates.

Over the past quarter century the purposes of performance appraisal have shifted. Before 1960, performance appraisals were most commonly used as control or administrative tools, supporting the activities of management. Since then, they have been used increasingly for personnel development and for planning purposes. More recently, following Equal Employment Opportunity legislation in the seventies, appraisals have been used to facilitate management decisions having EEO implications. In our respondents' companies, 91% conduct management level performance appraisals. The appraisals are used for compensation (85.6%), counseling (65.1%), training and development (64.3%), promotion (45.3%), manpower planning (43.1%), retention/discharge (30.3%), and validation of a selection technique (17.2%).

Appraisals are conducted most usually for lower and mid-level managers. Fewer than 48% of our respondents extended the appraisal program to top level management.

The appraising is typically conducted by a person's immediate superior, although others often contribute inputs.

Performance appraisal was found to be a process with five elements. These include goal setting, job analysis, performance standards, performance appraisal and finally the feedback interview. The majority of our respondents stated that:

- Their organizations had clear and concise statements of purpose
- Goal setting was part of the performance appraisal process
- When developing goals for a job, goals of other jobs inside and outside the department are considered
- Job analyses are task based
- Job descriptions delineate responsibilities, general objectives, tasks, knowledge, skill and ability
- Standards or specific goals of performance are developed for each major segment of individual jobs and negotiated between superior and subordinate

- Performance appraisal techniques used most frequently and perceived as most important included goal or standard setting, written essay statements and descriptions of critical incidents
- Appraisals have at least a moderately positive effect on leadership, productivity and efficiency.

Survey and interview findings indicated that:

- Greater emphasis should be placed on job analyses, to ensure the adequacy and legality of the performance appraisal process. All too often job analyses and resulting job descriptions are dated or non-existent
- Performance appraisal techniques should stress quantification and replicability
- Performance appraisals used for compensation and development purposes are best discussed with the appraised individual at separate times
- Consideration should be given to the difficulty of appraising staff versus line jobs, and the evaluation of members of the extended work force
- Performance appraisals should be conducted annually at a minimum, and more frequently when possible.
- It would be desirable to expand the appraisal process into an integrated human resource system

1

Performance Appraisal: An Overview

PERFORMANCE appraisal has been called the Achilles heel of management. Meidan (1981) has noted that "performance appraisal within the organization itself is generally acknowledged as one of the weakest points in organizational development.... Only recently have we begun to develop accurate ways of finding out whether practicing managers are really competent in their jobs." Even though many individuals have taken varying stands on what the "right" way of appraising performance is, it would appear that we have not really progressed very far.

During the Wei Dynasty, third century A.D., an "Imperial Rater" evaluated the performance of the members of the official family. His method of appraisal was subjective. In fact, there is a quote from a Chinese philosopher, Sin Yu, who criticized the system by stating: "the Imperial Rater of Nine Grades seldom rates men according to their merits, but always according to his likes and dislikes." In our present work environments, unfortunately, Sin Yu's criticism is still too often applicable.

At the present time, three facts are evident:

- Performance appraisal is an issue.
- No industry or academician has comprehensively solved the problems in performance appraisal.
- No two people agree completely on how to solve the issue.

The purpose of this research report is not to tell the reader about

RESEARCH METHODS

THIS study was based on literature review, a survey by mail, and personal interviews:

- The review of literature of the performance appraisal field was extensive. It encompassed two decades of publications, with particular attention to those of the most recent ten years.

- The questionnaire was designed to gain responses on those aspects of appraisal that appeared to be most critical as judged from the literature review. The questionnaire was mailed to a systematic sample of the members of the AMA Human Resources (N=832), Finance (N=665), Marketing (N=537) and Information Systems (N=366) Divisions. Of the 2400 questionnaires mailed, 588 were returned, representing a 24.5% return rate. A particularly detailed analysis was made of responses from representatives of those business firms which reported they have systems for appraising managers.

   Fifty-three percent of the respondents represented companies with gross revenues under $100 million. An additional 21.1 percent had revenues between $100 million and $499 million and 25.7% had revenues equal to or above $500 million. The respondents also varied according to the number of employees. Sixty percent of the sample had under 100 employees in their organizations, an additional 23.7 percent had between 100 and 4,999 employees, and the remaining 16.3 percent had 5000 or more employees.

   Respondents also provided specimens of current performance appraisal forms.

- Interviews were conducted with 12 respondents and performance appraisal specialists by telephone or in person. The interviews were planned to secure a greater depth of understanding of individual answers and patterns of replies observed in the survey responses.

a new and exciting way to conduct a performance appraisal, without any problems, but to provide:

- A current picture of performance appraisal in the business world.
- Examples of items used in the performance appraisal process.
- A review of the performance appraisal process.

- A user's checklist for evaluating existing and proposed performance appraisal systems.

For the present study, performance appraisal was defined as *the observation and assessment of employee performance against predetermined job-related standards, for the purpose(s) delineated by the organization.* Schick (1980) concurs with this definition, while Bush and Stinson (1980) and Olsen and Bennett (1975) would add that the purpose of the appraisal process is the improvement of performance. Most authors and practitioners seem to agree that it is the assessment of how well an employee is performing his/her job. The data obtained from the evaluation process can be used as input information for many activities and sub-programs in the organization.

Meidan (1981) has spelled out the objectives that managerial appraisal seeks to achieve:

> Generally speaking, the objectives of managerial appraisal are (1) to evaluate performers or improve performance in order to make promotion/dismissal/transfer decisions, review salaries, and identify training needs; (2) to allocate financial, production, technical, and marketing resources; (3) to aid in business planning; and (4) to make possible changes in organization and control systems.

He takes the position that the results of performance appraisal can and should serve more than one purpose in the host organization.

EVOLVING PURPOSES OF APPRAISAL

Before 1960, performance evaluations were designed primarily as tools for the organization to use in controlling employees. Past performance was used to guide or justify management's actions in dealing with the employee (Brinkerhoff & Kanter, 1980; Cummings, 1980; Sloan & Johnson, 1968). Performance appraisal provided the basis for salary and retention, discharge, or promotion decisions.

In the 1960's, the purpose of performance appraisal broadened to include development of the individual, organizational planning, and improving the quality of work life. Management now used performance appraisal to try to increase employees' productivity, effectiveness, efficiency, and satisfaction (Brinkerhoff & Kanter, 1980). Performance appraisal provided a basis for development of employee job skills, career planning, and motivation through effective coaching and information exchange between appraiser and appraisee.

Another shift in the purpose of performance appraisal occurred in the seventies. This was caused by legal pressures, requiring organizations to document and justify, for Equal Employment Opportunity purposes, all administrative actions (salary, promotion, and retention or discharge). Performance appraisal could explain and justify an organization's decisions by strengthening them with data in an orderly record (Beacham, 1979; Ford & Jennings, 1977).

Though these purposes can be viewed on a historical timeline, it must be emphasized that performance appraisal currently exists in organizations for one or more of the following reasons identified in surveys: administrative, developmental, and/or legal purposes. More than 85.6% of the respondents in the present survey use performance appraisal for compensation purposes. Nearly two companies out of three use appraisal for counseling (65.1%) and training and development (64.3%). Other purposes are promotion (45.3%), manpower planning (43.1%), retention/discharge (30.3%), and validation of a selection technique (17.2%).

These findings are consistent with the findings of others. Hay Associates (1975) in a survey of readers of its monthly publication found that 81% of the respondents (N = 853 organizations) used performance appraisal for (at least) compensation decisions when evaluating management level employees. Further, 54% of the responding organizations used it for manpower planning and training and development of these employees. Locher & Teel (1977) found similar results in their survey of organizations belonging to the Personnel

Exhibit 1. Purposes for Which Responding Companies Use Performance Evaluation

Purpose	Percentage of Those Responding
Compensation	85.6%
Counselling	65.1
Training & development	64.3
Promotion	45.3
Manpower planning	43.1
Retention/discharge	30.3
Validation of selection technique	17.2

and Industrial Relations Association. Seventy-one percent of their respondents (153 organizations) used performance appraisal for compensation decisions, 55% for performance improvement programs, and 11% for documentation purposes.

A FUNCTION OF HUMAN RESOURCES

Responsibility for planning for performance appraisal and for keeping the system in operation is usually assigned to the Human Resources/Personnel Department. Where the responsibility is placed within the department varies with the size and nature of the organization. In the larger companies, which tend to have larger human resources staffs, there is increased likelihood that the performance appraisal system will be the main responsibility of one manager.

Among our survey respondents, 424, representing 91% of the for-profit organizations participating, have a performance appraisal process of evaluating management-level personnel. Responsibility for these programs is centralized in 71% of the respondent companies. Responsibility for performance appraisal programs is decentralized to company divisions or subsidiaries in 26% of the responding companies. Exhibit 2 gives further details as to decentralization of appraisal programs.

WHO PARTICIPATES

Performance appraisals may be conducted for all levels of the workforce, from the lowest rank to the highest in the corporation. In practice, appraisals are often conducted with varying degrees of detail or thoroughness. At the lower levels comprising some of the larger numbers in the workforce, union preference for seniority-based decisions and standardized pay increases reduces emphasis on or perceived need for a complete appraisal of each individual. At the top levels, the assessment may be chiefly based on how well the reporting subunit or the total corporation has achieved its financial objectives.

Who Is Appraised

Our survey findings verify these impressions of the prevalence of performance appraisals at various levels. The respondents indicated

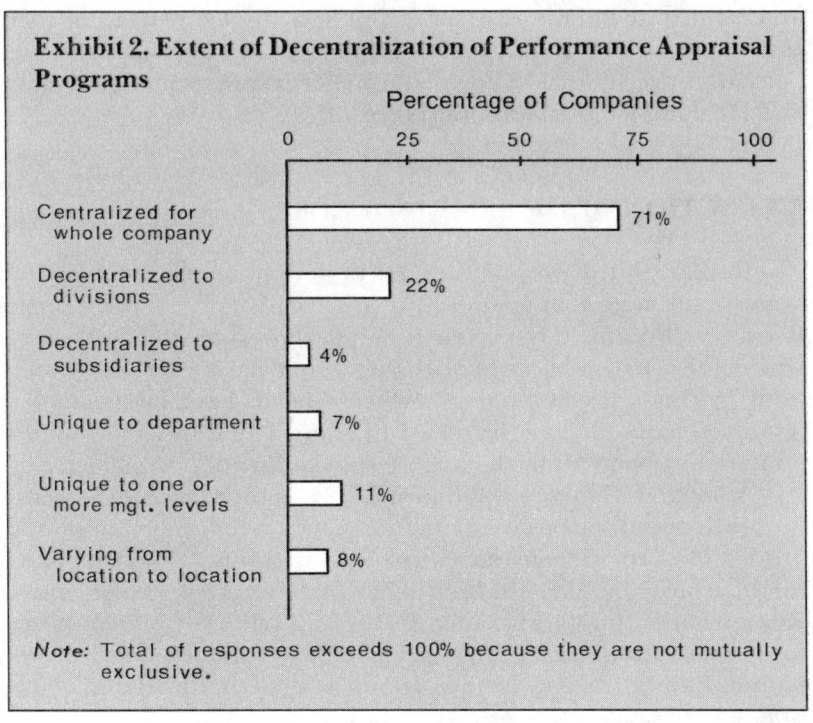

Exhibit 2. Extent of Decentralization of Performance Appraisal Programs

that in 41% of their organizations there were no programs for appraisal of non-management personnel. In contrast, only 27.4% of the responding companies lacked appraisal programs for lower level managers and an even lower 21.8% of the organizations lacked appraisal of middle level managers. Fully 52.4% of our respondent organizations did not have a performance appraisal program in place to evaluate members of their upper level management team.

Interview information suggests some of the reasons for the pattern of use of appraisals. There is a strong focus on appraisal of supervisors, managers, and other professionals because of the significant influence that this small band of individuals is perceived to have on the success of the company. Identification and advancement of effective supervisors, junior and middle managers and key technical people is seen as important. Their individual strengths and needs for training and development vary widely and need to be assessed separately. Further, their chiefs are likely to have received training in management, including appraisals; they also have relatively small spans of control, and can give attention to each subordinate.

Top officers are a special case. Their contributions are critical, but their reviews and salary and incentive compensation records have tended to be kept separate from those of others in the company. The CEO and other top-level appraisers are given extra latitude in the means used in their evaluations.

At the non-exempt level of production employees and junior clerks, the numbers are large and, especially in union-organized shops, the opportunity to recognize varying levels of effort or effectiveness with different rates of pay and different kinds of training is limited. Where appraisal is used, it is not uncommon to use simplified forms.

Individuals in both line and staff assignments are appraised, and field as well as home office personnel are appraised. This offers a challenge in the consistent application of standards. As Dr. William H. Bleuel, a partner in the management consulting firm of Zarkov and Gordon, noted in an interview:

> Though staff personnel have clear objectives and are appraised directly by supervisors, they may suffer by not being able to connect their objectives directly to organizational objectives in quantitative terms. Most line people, in contrast, may easily have their work appraised against quantitative production output and cost standards in situations where their work is regularly observed by superiors and peers.
>
> Members of the extended workforce—sales and service personnel, adjusters, etc. in the field—may not be seen in action by their supervisors on a daily basis, so they tend to be appraised on the basis of statistics, the impressions left by brief superior-subordinate contacts, and inputs from others external to the work group or even external to the organization. Systems for objective measurement of performance in the extended workforce environment are sometimes rather inadequate.

Who Does the Appraising

It is no surprise to find from our survey that the employee's immediate supervisor virtually always takes a major role in the appraisal. Only 2.2% of the respondents say that the immediate supervisor does *not* take part in appraisals in their companies. The super-

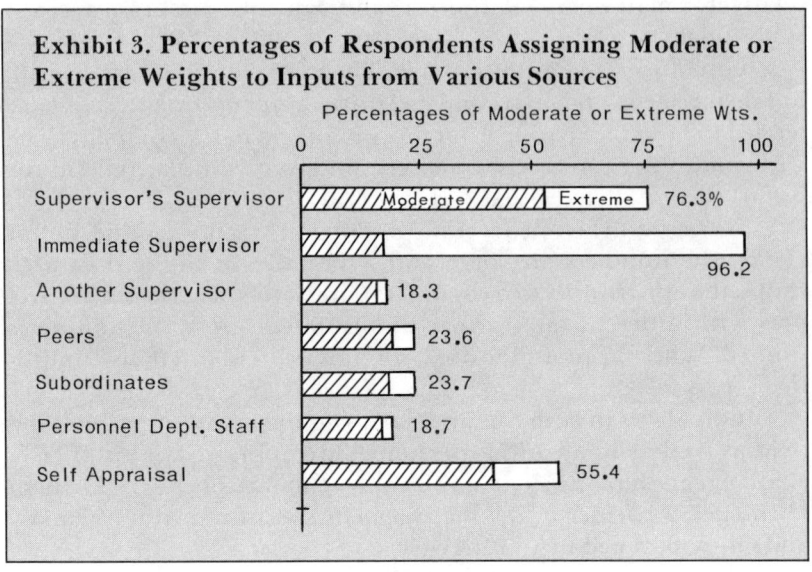

visor's supervisor also takes part in the appraisal in almost as many of the companies reporting. Only 8.0% of the respondents say that this next-level supervisor does *not* participate. Involvement of others is not nearly as usual: in 63% of the companies, another supervisor joins in the appraisal to some degree; in 53%, someone from the personnel department staff takes part in one way or another; and in about half of the companies, some input (usually described as "slight") comes from the employee's peers or subordinates. In three out of four companies, respondents say there is either informal or formal input from the appraisee—that is, self-appraisal.

Survey participants were asked to estimate the influence of appraisal inputs from the several categories of participants. They reported whether "slight," "moderate," or "extreme" would be the appropriate word to use to describe the weight typically given to the appraisal input from each source. Exhibit 3 charts their responses. For simplicity, the percentages of answers of moderate and extreme have been totalled.

The influence of the immediate supervisor stands out, with 78.9% of the respondents reporting that this individual's input is given extreme weight in an appraisal and 17.3% that it is given moderate weight—for a total of 96.2%. The supervisor's supervisor is seen as next in influence, with 23.0% of our respondents saying that the weight given to this next-level supervisor's input is extreme and 53.3% that it is moderate—for a total of 76.3%. The weight given to inputs from others acquainted with the appraisee's work (other supervisors, peers, subordinates, personnel department staff) is rarely described as extreme, and is described as moderate by only 16-19% of the survey respondents.

THE PERFORMANCE APPRAISAL PROCESS

The fit of performance appraisal into an organization is best understood after some preliminary discussion of elements critical to the organization as well as to the performance appraisal process itself. These elements include goal setting, job analysis, performance standards and performance feedback. They are essential parts of an integrated performance evaluation process.

Goal Setting

Goal setting translates organizational goals into divisional, departmental, and finally into specific job objectives, from a top down perspective. Goal setting begins with a clear and concise statement of the purpose of the organization—the mission. The mission provides the basis for the formulation of long range organizational goals and strategic plans. It also focuses management's attention on needs; it helps to identify and define key areas of organizational performance and activity.

The mission of the organization answers questions about the current business, customers, overall strategy, structure and environment, return on investment, and the contributions to the community at large (Raia, 1974). The statements of corporate goals and strategic plans are more precise than the mission statements. There is an iterative process of establishing major long range goals of the organization and specifying the way in which resources will be employed to achieve them.

The overall goals specify the performance, activities and results to be accomplished by the total organization within a given time span. They cover both the economic and non-economic areas of the organization. Goals are based upon the identification of key areas of which the following are representative: profitability, markets, productivity, product, financial resources, physical facilities, research and innovation, organizational structure, human resources, and social responsibility.

From these goals more specific objectives are identified and defined for the major divisions, departments, and subunits of an organization. This continues downward through the organizational hierarchy so that goals and objectives permeate the whole organizational structure as well as the management process, providing an underpinning for planning efforts, direction, motivation and control (Richards, 1978).

In the present study, 72% of the respondents stated that their organization had a clear and concise statement of purpose. Eighty-two percent stated that goal setting was part of their performance evaluation process. Eighty percent stated that the goals for departments and subunits are derived from the company goals. More than 80% of the respondents stated that when developing goals for a job, goals of jobs in the department are considered as are goals of jobs in other departments.

After the organizational goals have been translated into a goal structure for a unit, the responsibilities which have the most impact on the success of the organization and on the success of the individual performing the job must be delineated.

Job Analysis

The second element, job analysis, focuses on the component tasks of jobs, at every level, associated with achievement of a goal or a set of goals. These tasks derive from specific sets of activities. At the managerial level they may include planning, organizing, controlling, directing and leading, communicating, staffing, negotiating, developing one's self, and decision making. At the secretarial level, activities may include answering the phone, typing, arranging appointments and meetings, filing, etc.

A more recent approach to the study of the employee in the workplace involves the identification of the specific competencies needed to fulfill the responsibilities of a certain job. Such competencies can be isolated for each job, and hence worker, in the organization.

A job is defined as some series of tasks to be performed—tasks which are usually structured by the subunit (department) of the organization. Job analysis is the process of studying and collecting information pertaining to the task elements, operations, and responsibilities of a specific job (Flippo, 1980; Klinger, 1979). Job analysis should be an ongoing activity which uncovers, synthesizes, and disseminates information about jobs that can be used in decisions relating to organizational planning and design, human resources management, and other managerial functions (Ghorpage and Atchison, 1980).

There are three approaches to job analysis: task oriented, worker oriented, and abilities oriented. The task oriented approach breaks down each job into elemental units called tasks (Dunnette and Kirchner, 1959; Morsh, 1964; Zavala, 1980). Although the definition of what constitutes a task varies among authors, the focus of the analysis is always upon the elements of the work activity itself.

In the worker-oriented job analysis the units of analysis are the generalized human behaviors required to do the work (McCormick, 1979). Using this approach, similarities and differences among jobs are described in terms of processes that are common to all jobs, and are not idiosyncratic to the particular job or job family (McCormick, Jeanneret and Mecham, 1972).

The third type of job analysis is the abilities oriented approach in which the units of analysis are profiles of abilities or competencies required to perform the work (Fleishman, 1972, 1975). Fleishman developed a taxonomy of psychomotor abilities, physical proficiency abilities and cognitive abilities that are necessary for task performance. Henderson (1980) noted that the higher (more complex cognitive) the level of the job, the more important the cognitive and affective domains become and the less important the psychomotor domains.

Each of these different approaches stresses some different important aspect of work. Since different aspects of work are examined with each approach, it is entirely possible to reach different conclusions about the similarities and differences among jobs, depending upon the type of job analysis data that was collected. However, not much is known about the superiority of one particular job analysis technique over another (Dunham, 1978; Dunham and Taylor, 1980; Prien and Ronan, 1971). Perhaps the major conclusion found in the literature on job analysis is that the job analyst should be familiar with, and where appropriate use, several methods of job analysis (Brumback and Vincent, 1970; Levine, Ash and Bennett, 1980).

Sixty percent of the organizations participating in this study stated that the job analyses they perform are task based; twenty-seven percent performed behavior-based job analyses.

Performance appraisal is linked to job analysis with varying degrees of formality. For example, Vincent Conte, supervisor-compensation of the Insurance Services Office (New York) commented in an interview:

> Our performance appraisals are not based directly on the results of the job analysis. When job analyses are performed, they result in finalized job descriptions. The job analyses and job descriptions are then used in the initial selection and filtering process as the job is being filled. The job descriptions are available to all levels of managers so they can use the descriptions and various descriptors in developing and negotiating the goals and objectives for the individual employee.

Job Descriptions

Regardless of the approach, the primary output of a job analysis is a job description. Generally, the description constitutes a record of existing and pertinent job facts. The record usually includes three categories of information; job missions and location, work performed (job elements), and the environmental context of the job.

Klinger (1979) states that job descriptions would be more useful if they clarified the organization's expectations of employees and the linkages between tasks, standards, skills and minimum qualifications. Klinger calls these "results oriented job descriptions." He states that a results oriented job description focuses on the performance standards, the conditions that differentiate jobs and the linkages between standards, skills, knowledge, abilities and qualifications.

The present study found that 89% of the respondents had job descriptions which delineated responsibilities; 84% delineated general objectives and purposes; 75%, tasks; 72%, knowledge, skill and abilities. Further details are given in Exhibit 4.

Performance Standards and Appraisal

Regardless of the appraisal technique selected, the content should be based on standards of performance. Standards of performance represent the level of results needed to ensure the accomplishment of the organization's goals. The combination of one's job standards with standards of other jobs in the department comprise the department's standards. The combination of standards of all departments

Exhibit 4. Focus of the Job Analysis

	Not Applic.	Agree			Disagree	
		Strongly	Moderately	Neutral	Moderately	Strongly
Focuses on						
Behaviors	22.8%	3.9%	23.2%	20.9%	21.3%	7.9%
Tasks	14.0	13.6	46.9	16.7	6.2	2.7
States						
Responsibilities	5.1	42.2	46.9	2.3	3.1	0.4
Objectives and purposes	4.7	39.5	44.5	5.1	5.5	0.8
Results in job description which states						
Tasks	5.1	30.6	44.7	9.4	8.6	1.6
Knowledge, skills, abilities	7.8	29.0	43.1	11.4	7.1	1.6

provides the organization with the ability to accomplish its goals. Standards of performance should be developed with the same vertical and horizontal integration as in the goal setting process.

As mentioned previously, the appraisal form should be designed to ascertain how well the employee's actual performance meets the standards of performance. The results of the appraisal feed back into the definition of the goals, and the cycle begins again. One procedure for feeding back the information into the system is by means of a performance review.

Our survey responses, presented in Exhibit 5, indicate that 55.5% of the respondents stated that a series of standards or specific goals of performance is developed for each major segment of individual jobs. Almost fifty-eight percent stated that standards of performance are developed through negotiations between supervisor and subordinate and are included in the organizations performance appraisal program. Just under seventy percent stated that performance standards are linked to departmental objectives.

PROBLEM AREAS

Experience reported in the prior literature indicates that performance appraisals tend to fail when they are used for more than one purpose (Cummings, 1980; Fournies, 1974; Ralph, 1980). When a

Exhibit 5. Characteristics of Performance Standards

	Not Applic.	Agree			Disagree	
		Strongly	Moderately	Neutral	Moderately	Strongly
Standards are						
Linked to departmental objectives	5.8%	22.2%	47.5%	15.6%	7.8%	1.2%
Developed for each major segment of individual's job	11.6	20.2	35.3	14.3	15.5	3.1
Negotiated between empl. & supv. and incl. in performance evaluation program	9.3	16.3	41.5	12.0	17.8	3.1

company uses the performance appraisal for administrative decisions—particularly pay and promotion decisions—whatever developmental impetus the system is intended to have is lost (Brinkerhoff & Kanter, 1980).

Adverse Effects of Multiple Uses

This is illustrated in a classic study by Meyer, Kay and French (1965). They investigated how the purpose of appraisal affected the ratees. They found that counselling an employee on developmental issues when he or she knows a salary increase hangs on a favorable evaluation is usually ineffective. The tension leads the employee to be defensive and to blame other people or other factors for any shortcomings pointed out. Indeed, because of the stress involved in the interview, the appraisee may even fail to remember critical incidents discussed and recommendations made.

Meyer et al. and many others recommend separating evaluation for salary administration purposes from evaluation to improve performance or to plan for development. They argue that a performance appraisal should have only one purpose or else it will fail to accomplish its goals.

Nevertheless, our current survey reconfirms that business firms commonly use performance appraisals for multiple purposes. Details are given in Exhibit 6.

One could wish the literature offered an integrative way of con-

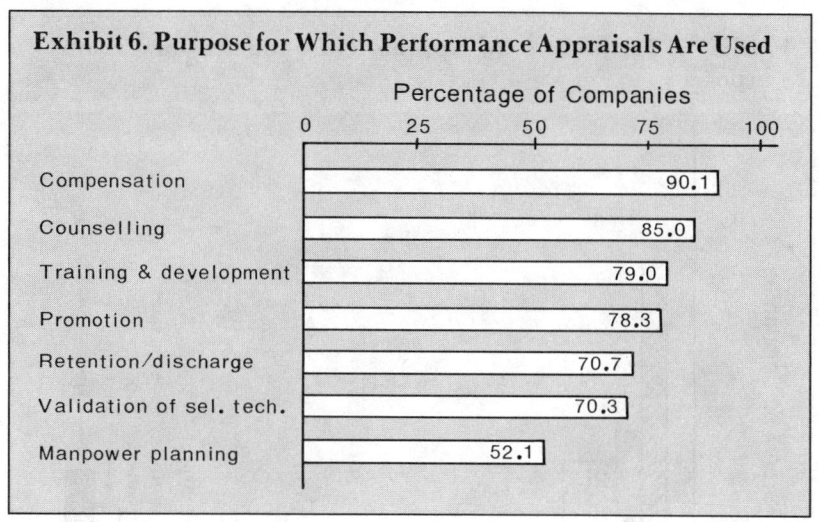

ducting and utilizing appraisals for more than one purpose—a solution that would aid organizations with their multiple needs. Instead, it chooses to take the position that organizations should conduct multiple appraisals for various purposes. This solution may, however, be seen as too time consuming and costly in some cases. Perhaps a more appropriate solution may be to collect appraisal information once, but discuss compensation and development issues at different times.

There is some indication in our data that many companies *do* separate the *times* for appraisals used for different purposes. For example, as Exhibit 7 shows, 77.7% of the companies surveyed conduct appraisals for compensation purposes on an annual basis, and only relatively small percentages of companies conduct them at other intervals. In contrast, markedly less companies (39.2% and 45.3%, respectively) report that they make appraisals for counselling and training/development purposes on an annual basis. Instead, many conduct their appraisals for these purposes at semiannual, quarterly or other intervals. And in some cases known to the authors, salary reviews and developmental evaluations are conducted at different times of the year even though each is an annual event.

Edward F. Walsh, vice president, personnel at PepsiCo Inc., told us in an interview:

> We tie our performance appraisals to salary increases, and we do the

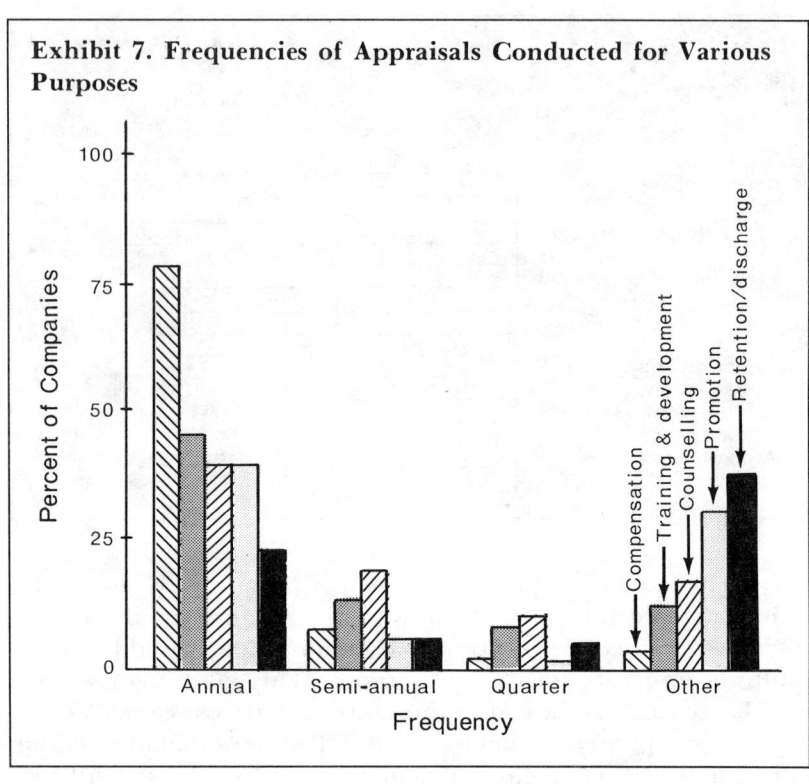

Exhibit 7. Frequencies of Appraisals Conducted for Various Purposes

appraisals at whatever time period is appropriate. We work very hard to separate the performance appraisal [for compensation] from the performance evaluation used in our human resource planning process. It's very important to separate the two. In fact, if you really were to look at the sequence of events for our middle managers, you would find they get three appraisals a year. They get a salary appraisal keyed to their accountabilities. For incentive pay purposes, they get a second appraisal, probably keyed to specific goals they helped to set. And the third appraisal is part of the human resources review plan.

And Robert Schreiber, vice president of technology management at Salomon Brothers Inc, added:

Up until a year or so ago, we used to give the annual appraisals within a week of giving bonuses. We found that people concentrated on the compensation and didn't really pay much attention to the development side of the appraisal. What we planned to do this year was give the appraisals a couple of months earlier so we could separate the time of sitting down in the [developmental] appraisal interview from the time two months later that we talked strictly about compensation.

Almost all use of appraisals for salary purposes is at fixed intervals, while appraisals for other purposes are often made on a flexible or "when appropriate" basis. Appraisals for counselling and development/training purposes are made more frequently than compensation appraisals—either semiannually or quarterly—in about one company out of four. And the use of appraisals at still other intervals—particularly on a variable or "when appropriate" basis—rises in successive jumps for those made for development/training, counselling, promotion, and retention/discharge purposes.

As will be further explained in a later section, a justificatory function for appraisal has been taking on greater significance in an environment of pressures for equal employment opportunity and affirmative action (Schneier, 1978). The courts are beginning to set requirements for an organization's performance appraisal program, though their standards are by no means comprehensive as yet.

Taking all this into account, companies are asking: "What should be the purpose of performance appraisal?" Should appraisal rate employee performance (for pay and other administrative decisions), improve it (the developmental purpose), or justify organizational personnel decisions? Companies are now left with the job of reconciling at least three potentially conflicting purposes.

One way in which companies have dealt with this is by zeroing in on its major purpose or purposes and then selecting an appropriate appraisal technique or techniques to match. This still requires quite a bit of trial and error, as there appears to be no substantial research that demonstrates systematically which approach works best for which purpose. Instead, the research has generally focused on how well the various techniques minimize certain rater biases.

Unexpected Requirements

Another problem is the standard that catches the individual by surprise in the appraisal interview. Such situations arise mainly from poor communication, some of which may be inherent in a particular appraisal system.

In one version of the problem, the appraised individual is told he or she has not displayed a good level of, say, cooperation or initiative. The appraisee disagrees. An argument follows. This situation is especially likely to occur with appraisal systems that rate personal traits or rather generalized behaviors.

To reduce such difficulties, many companies have been moving toward appraisal techniques that emphasize more specific on-the-job results and outcomes. These are negotiated or at least identified early in the work period. Coaching discussions during the period also help to clarify the supervisor's expectations.

In the second form of the problem, the difficulty comes from changes in job targets or priorities. At appraisal time the individual may be downrated for not having reached a goal or solved a particular problem. The appraisee argues that this target was never made clear.

Robert Schreiber, vice president of Salomon Brothers, illustrated the way this may come about, and indicated how the difficulty may be minimized:

> As the business changes or new opportunities come up that the business wants to develop, people's objectives are going to change. Within a period of days, priorities will be juggled so that even if I had said "Developing System A is the highest priority," two weeks later that priority might change. ... Subordinates' activities will shift almost as quickly, but the changes may not be reflected immediately in their performance plans. ... One of our ground rules for the performance planning process is that we expect managers to sit down periodically with each employee for a discussion (not the official appraisal) of how the manager feels the employee is performing against the plan and how the employee feels he is doing against the plan, and make changes to reflect real activity. All you have to do is put a handwritten note on the plan that a given objective is changed for the following reason. ... We focus on getting the hot thing done, and then if we get to changing the plan, fine; if not, we allow for the change at appraisal time.

Legal Context

The performance appraisal method employed has increasingly come under scrutiny and review from the equal employment opportunity (EEO) viewpoint. Recent legislation has affected two areas related to performance appraisals: staffing and employee compensation. The results of performance appraisal can serve as criteria for validating selection procedures used in staffing decisions or as tests used as a basis for employment decisions involving transfer and promotion, demotion, compensation, layoff, termination, and selection for training programs.

The legal context of performance appraisal was altered as a result of the Tower Amendment of the 1964 Civil Rights Act (Title VII). This amendment approved the use of "professionally developed ability tests" for employment decisions, provided such tests were not designed, intended, or used to discriminate because of race, color, religion, sex, or national origin (Siegel, 1980).

The Equal Employment Opportunity Commission (EEOC) was given legislative responsibility for enforcing this act (Title VII). In 1966, the EEOC issued guidelines regarding an employer's obligation for testing and selection procedures pertaining to equal employment opportunity. These guidelines were revised in 1970 and again in 1978.

In 1971, the Supreme Court's decision in Griggs vs. Duke Power incorporated the guidelines into a legal framework for employment testing. To assess the possible adverse impact of a selection procedure, EEOC recommends that it be validated for each minority group for which it is used.

Where the requirement of a high school education or the passing of a standardized general intelligence test or other requirements for employment or promotion have been found to be unrelated to the needs of the job, they have been judged arbitrary and discriminatory. The Court has required employers to demonstrate nondiscrimination when it appears that a selection requirement has an adverse impact on a minority group. Performance appraisal ratings are often used as the criterion against which a selection requirement is tested to prove job relatedness.

In Brito vs. Zia Company (1973), the Court stated that Zia Company had violated Title VII when on the basis of poor performance ratings, it laid off several Spanish surnamed employees. The Court concluded that the practice was illegal since:

- The evaluations were based on subjective supervisory observation
- The evaluations caused a disproportionate reduction in the number of Spanish-surnamed employees
- The evaluations were not administered and scored in a controlled and standardized manner
- Two of the three supervisory evaluators did not have daily contact with the employees being evaluated.

On the basis of the evidence the Court received, it concluded that the evaluations were based on the "best judgments and opinions" of evaluators, but not on any identifiable objective criterion which was supported by some kind of record. As a result, the court decided that Zia had failed to produce sufficient evidence of validity for its performance appraisal system.

The significance of this case is that the courts equated performance appraisals with tests. Hence, the performance appraisal system employed by Zia Company was required to meet EEOC guidelines on employee selection procedures.

In 1975, the Court addressed performance appraisals as criteria for the validation of a pre-employment test in the case of Albermarle Paper Company vs. Moody. The Court found that Albermarle's validation was based on test scores being compared to "vague and questionable standards of supervisory ratings." The significance of this case was that the Court decided that there had been no job analysis and that the validation sample was unrepresentative of the potential job applicants who would take the test.

In Wade vs. Mississippi Cooperative Extension Service (1976), the Court addressed the issue of promotion and concluded that the appraisal instrument used by the state agricultural extension service for appraisal of professional employees was insufficiently job related. The Court concluded that there was discrimination on the part of the evaluating supervisors. In addition, there was sufficient evidence to indicate that the scores were not used consistently as a cause for promoting employees or establishing their salaries. Finally, the Mississippi Cooperative Extension Service could not demonstrate to the satisfaction of the Court that the appraisal instrument was substantially related to the particular job(s) of the individuals being evaluated.

On August 25, 1978, Uniform Guidelines on Employee Selection Procedures were adopted by the Equal Employment Opportunity Commission, the Civil Service Commission, the Department of Justice, and the Department of Labor. These Uniform Guidelines replaced existing requirements and have provided one consistent set of federal regulations. The Guidelines include the following statements:

- Employers may not, through the use of any selection device for employment decisions, discriminate against any group protected under Title VII of the Civil Rights Act of 1964

- Employment decisions are any personnel practices which result in selection, training, transfer, retention or promotion of employees
- It is not necessary to establish an intent to discriminate to prove discrimination. The presence (or absence) of a disproportionate number from a protected group is defined as prima facie evidence of discrimination (DeVries et al., 1980).

Further, the Guidelines do not require validation documentation in all cases—just those cases where the test or selection device (e.g. performance appraisal ratings) results in adverse impact on a protected group (DeVries et al., 1980).

During the past decade the courts have addressed a number of uses and aspects of performance appraisal (e.g. employment practices involving transfers, promotions, and training programs). Several authors have reviewed the guidelines and recent court cases involving performance appraisal and have drawn conclusions about the criteria upon which the courts may judge performance appraisals in the eighties (Field and Holley, 1981; Kleiman and Durham, 1981; Lubben, Thompson, and Klasson, 1980; Odom, 1977).

For a defensible performance appraisal system, the performance appraisal ratings (administration and scoring) should be formalized, standardized, and as objective as possible. The appraisal should be job related by being based on a formal job analysis. If the appraisal involves multiple measures of performance, a fixed weight should be assigned to each measure with respect to the overall assessment.

When objective data are used, an employer should be able to demonstrate that such appraisal ratings are uncontaminated (i.e., the level of performance is uninfluenced by factors outside the control of the employee) and nondeficient (i.e., all important aspects of job behavior are reflected in the objective record) (Kleiman and Durham, 1981).

If objective data are not used, then two suggestions have been offered for the use of subjective ratings. Only qualified raters should be used in the rating process. A qualified rater is someone who has sufficient opportunity to observe the appraisee and is trained in how to conduct the appraisal. The rating scale should be based on job behaviors, not attributes of the employees. Regardless of the type of data used in the appraisal, objective or subjective, all employees should be given feedback on their performances.

Although quite a few authors are showing extreme concern over the legal attacks on performance appraisal systems, some of the results of the present survey suggest that this concern is not shared by many companies. For example, less than half the survey respondents (46.2%) have a training program in the appraisal process. Three out of five (60.1%) of our respondents believed the essay technique, which is subjective and often based on personal traits, is very or extremely important to the appraisal process. These results are similar to those of earlier studies in the field. Lazer and Wikstrom (1977) indicated that fewer than half of the 217 companies surveyed had developed their appraisal systems on the basis of a job analysis and over 60% use personal traits when assessing an employee's performance. The Bureau of National Affairs survey (1974) indicated that for managerial personnel, 52% of 139 companies gave no training in applying appraisal techniques. Some 64% used personality traits on their rating forms and one of the employers did not offer feedback to the employee (Basnight and Wolkinson, 1977).

It is the opinion of the researchers that, during the next decade, organizations will be revising their appraisal systems so as to comply with federal guidelines or else many of them will risk being found guilty of employment discrimination. The most helpful source of information on this so far is the book by Plumlee, Machemehl and Utter (1983).

As organizations decide to review their systems, and seek help from the literature, they will find weaknesses. The literature overwhelms the reader with information on the various elements of evaluation systems, such as goal setting, job analysis, standards of performance, techniques, and performance review interviews. It is not yet as helpful as one could wish in integrating these concepts into a unified model or concept which has application in organizations. One is much needed. If it is agreed that the role of the Human Resources/Personnel staff is to create and develop effective policies and programs that attract, retain and motivate employees, they would seem to be logical individuals to contribute such a model. Consideration must be given to the primary human resources activities of:

- Recruiting and selecting employees
- Administering these programs in accordance with equal rights and federal legislation
- Development and maintenance of organizational development programs based on most recent behavioral science fundings

- Human resources planning and administration
- Development and training
- Compensation
- Employee benefit programs
- Personnel records administration.

The important question to start with is: "What role do performance appraisals currently have in the human resource process?" Instead of a well considered system of human resource needs matched with processes, appraisals appear to be a "one shot" tool in a large number of organizations. As indicated by our respondents, in many cases they are conducted annually on the employee's anniversary date for compensation and development, with feedback discussed in a single performance interview.

2

Performance Appraisal Techniques

OUR SURVEY also explored the appraisal techniques used by the private sector respondents whose companies have a performance evaluation program for managers. This part of the report will concentrate on the techniques available for the performance appraisal process and found to be in use in the field. Study of the techniques seems warranted because of their variety and the subtleties and complexities they involve. While job analysis and performance standards can be considered the bedrock of performance appraisal, the appraisal and feedback techniques are the core of the process. The technique selected can fortify or undermine the effectiveness of the appraisal activity. It can raise or lower the probability of obtaining objective information or quantitative data. This in turn will influence the likelihood that an appraisal system will withstand the scrutiny of an Equal Employment Opportunity inquiry.

The questionnaire presented a list of sentences describing tools or techniques often used in connection with performance appraisal. The respondents were asked to check the ones used in connection with the performance evaluation process in their companies. The sentences gave definitions for a series of techniques or tools identified in the literature by short labels such as "graphic rating scales," "ranking," "forced choices," etc. Exhibit 8 shows the relative usage reported for the various tools.

The tools whose use was most frequently mentioned were goal setting, written essay statements, description of critical incidents, and

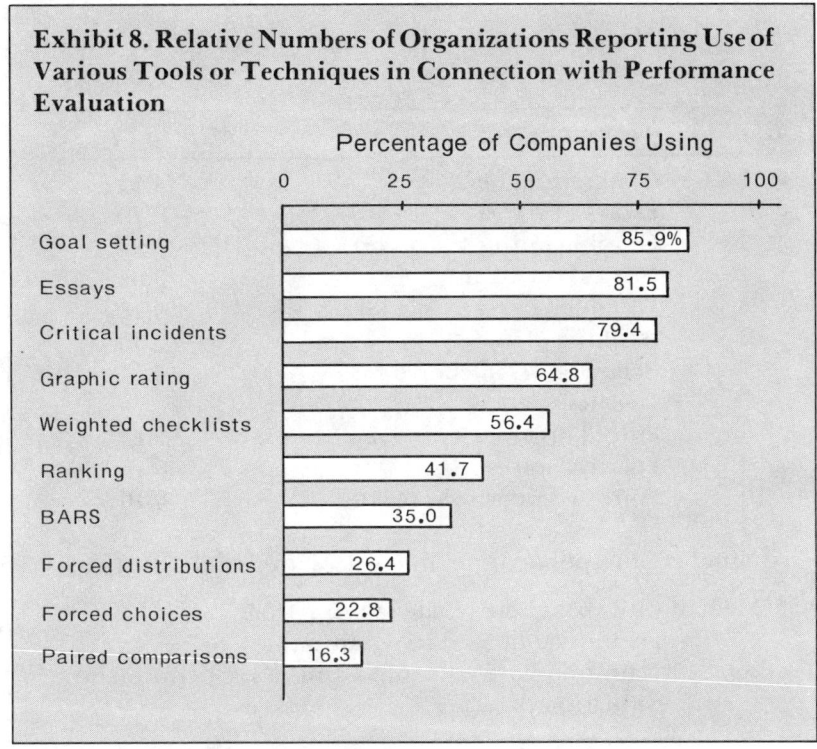

Exhibit 8. Relative Numbers of Organizations Reporting Use of Various Tools or Techniques in Connection with Performance Evaluation

graphic rating scales. Those used least were paired comparisons, forced choices and forced distributions.

Respondents also rated the importance of each tool or technique used in their companies' performance evaluation processes, on a scale of 1 to 5. As indicated in Exhibit 9, when scored by importance the various techniques appear in the same order except for graphic rating scales and critical incidents. The most interesting point here is the sharp difference in weights given to the upper four tools as compared with the lower six. Goal setting, essay-type statements, graphic rating scales and critical incidents stand out as much the most important in the perceptions of the respondents.

Clearly there is a whole range of tools and techniques available for use in the appraisal process. We will now look at these one at a time. For convenience, we will divide them into three categories: comparative, absolute, and outcome oriented. Comparative methods require the appraiser to evaluate the employees in a work unit relative to each other; absolute methods require the appraiser to evaluate the

Exhibit 9. Median Value of Importance of Each Technique to the Organization's Performance Evaluation Process

Rank	Technique (n)*	Median value**
1	Goal setting (452)	4.14
2	Essays (454)	3.79
3	Graphic rating scales (451)	3.27
4	Critical incidents (445)	3.07
5	Weighted checklists (448)	0.48
6	Ranking (450)	0.36
7	Behaviorally anchored rating scales (449)	0.27
8	Forced distributions (452)	0.18
9	Forced choices (452)	0.15
10	Paired comparisons (453)	0.10

*Number of respondents used in calculation of the median.

**Median value based on a scale ranging from:
  0 = technique not used in organizations, to
  5 = technique extremely important in the performance evaluation process.

employee without making direct reference to the other employees; and outcome oriented methods involve evaluating employees on the results they have achieved.

COMPARATIVE METHODS

There are three comparative methods: ranking, paired comparison, and forced choice.

Ranking

Ranking requires the rater to start at the top or bottom and list the employees in descending or ascending order on the trait being rated. Usually, one global overall performance trait is rated rather than separate specific traits (Flippo, 1980; Sanders & Peay, 1975). A global performance trait seeks to get at the employee's overall effectiveness to the organization. The employees are compared with respect to "their overall competence, the effectiveness with which they perform their jobs, their proficiency, their general overall value" (Mahoney, Sorenson, Verdee, and Nash, 1963).

Paired Comparisons

The paired comparison technique is a special form of simple ranking. The appraiser compares each person being evaluated with each other person being evaluated, one at a time. For each pair of persons, the rater chooses the one who ranks highest in the pair. For the whole series of comparisons, the number of times each person is "preferred" is calculated, and a ranking of all the individuals is made on the basis of this preference frequency (Bell, 1979; Cascio, 1978; Haynes, 1978).

Forced Distribution

Forced distribution begins by setting up categories from poor to good. The rater places names of the employees in the categories with the restriction that only a certain percentage of the people can be assigned to each category. The percentages are developed so that there is a quasi-normal distribution of people in the categories. This forces the rater to distribute the employees according to a pre-scaled scheme (Morano, 1974; Sanders & Peay, 1975).

Pros and Cons of Comparative Methods

According to Ghiselli and Brown (1955), there are two advantages to comparative methods: simplicity and naturalness.

> It is a very simple process to evaluate persons by merely arranging them in order from best to poorest or from most to least in terms of some characteristics. Furthermore, ranking is a very natural type of evaluation, involving a kind of judgment which is frequently made in everyday living. (p. 96)

There are several disadvantages to the comparative methods. First, comparative methods yield only an ordinal scale that permits a rank ordering of individuals without knowledge about the amount of difference between them (Anastasi, 1976). The techniques are limited by their inability to show relative distance on a performance dimension between two adjacent employees (Haynes, 1978; Ivancevich et al., 1980).

Second, the employees are usually compared only in terms of a single overall category of performance, and therefore, the ratings lack behavioral specificity. The ranking method does not give an accurate picture of the diversity of human resources, skills (e.g., mechanical or technical) and abilities (e.g., leadership or decision making) that are available in the work force of the organization (Cascio, 1978; Sanders and Peay, 1975). The organization only knows how its employees rank on some global assessment of overall effectiveness. This single rating limits the use of the appraisal to an administrative purpose because one does not know the specific areas of development needed for the employee.

Third, the task of ranking becomes more difficult for the evaluator as the number of employees to be appraised increases. According to Ivancevich et al. (1980), rankings of large groups of subordinates are less valid than rankings of small groups. Thus, even if the supervisor accomplishes the laborious task, the validity of the results is questionable.

The vast majority of our respondents indicated that the comparative methods are not very important in their performance appraisal systems. Their level of importance appeared related to the level of difficulty for implementation. Only 25.2% of the respondents considered ranking to be moderately to extremely important, while 10.1%

Exhibit 10. Importance of Comparative Methods As Perceived in Respondents' Companies

	Ranking	*Paired Comparisons*	*Forced Distribution*
Extremely important	3.9%	0.4%	4.3%
Very important	8.1	2.3	3.9
Moderately important	13.2	1.9	1.9
Slightly important	9.3	4.7	8.9
Not important	6.6	7.4	8.9
Not applic. in our co.	58.9	83.3	72.0

reported this level of importance for the forced distribution method, and only 4.6% for the paired comparison technique. Further details are presented in Exhibit 10.

ABSOLUTE METHODS

With absolute methods, the evaluator appraises the employee without resorting to direct comparisons with other employees. Techniques in this category include writing essay-type answers to questions about the employee's work and behavior, and the use of graphic rating scales, critical incidents, weighted checklists, or behaviorally anchored rating scales (BARS).

The Essay Approach

The narrative essay is a description of worker qualities and attitudes in the appraiser's own words. The rater is required to describe in writing an employee's strengths, weaknesses, and potential, together with suggestions for improvement. The assumption underlying this approach is that a candid statement from a rater who is knowledgeable of a ratee's performance is more concrete and just as valid as more formal and quantitative appraisal methods (Cascio, 1978).

As noted earlier, while essay responses are rather subjective and questionable in light of new employment legislation, 73.7% of our respondents considered the essay to be of moderate to extreme importance in their performance appraisal process. An example of an evaluation form using the essay approach is shown in Exhibit 11.

The advantage of narrative essays is that they can provide detailed, specific feedback to ratees regarding their performance. Since essays are almost totally unstructured and vary widely in length and content, two problems arise. First, comparisons across different employees are virtually impossible since different essays touch on different aspects of ratee performance or personal qualifications, even if the evaluations were written by the same appraiser (Sanders and Peay, 1975). Second, the employee's rating may depend as much on the writing skills of the evaluator as on the employee's performance (Ivancevich et al., 1980; Sanders and Peay, 1975). For these reasons, industry has been moving toward more quantitative, absolute techniques which involve behavioral content.

> **Exhibit 11. Example of Narrative Essay**
>
> Name: Department:
>
> Title: Time in Present Position:
>
> **PERFORMANCE HIGHLIGHTS**—Major accomplishments or important areas in which accomplishments exceeded or were less than expected.
>
>
>
>
> **EVALUATION OF MANAGEMENT SKILLS**—Person's ability to plan, organize, delegate, develop subordinates, etc.
>
>
>
>
> **PERSONAL STRENGTHS/AREAS NEEDING IMPROVEMENT**

Weighted Checklists

Two methods have developed from the behavioral content category: checklists and rating scales. Checklists were developed to aid the

Exhibit 12. Importance of Absolute Methods As Perceived in Respondents' Companies

	Essays	Weighted Checklist	Critical Incidents	Graphic Rating Scale	BARS
Extremely important	23.9%	6.3%	13.0%	19.3%	6.6%
Very important	38.6	18.0	28.0	28.2	9.4
Moderately important	11.2	13.3	16.9	9.7	7.0
Slightly important	6.2	3.9	11.8	4.2	3.1
Not important	4.2	6.3	5.5	2.7	4.7
Not applic. in our co.	15.8	52.3	24.8	35.9	69.1

appraiser in consistently comparing and ranking certain criteria for personnel decisions. When using a behavioral checklist, the rater is provided with a series of descriptive statements of job-related behavior. The rater indicates (by a checkmark) which statements are descriptive of the ratee or what degree each statement is descriptive of the ratee.

In the literature, the most common checklist technique is the weighted checklist. As can be seen in Exhibit 12, 37.6% of our respondents say the weighted checklist is from moderately to extremely important in their appraisal systems. The weighted checklist consists of a number of statements describing various types and levels of behavior for a particular job or group of jobs. Weights are assigned to each statement by a group of persons (e.g. the supervisors of the jobs to be appraised) based on how favorable or unfavorable it is for successful performance. The rater indicates the extent to which each statement describes the employee being evaluated. The checkmarks and their corresponding weights are summed up for each subordinate (Bell, 1979; Ivancevich et al., 1980). An example of a weighted checklist is given in Exhibit 13.

Critical Incidents

Another behaviorally oriented checklist, regarded as moderately to extremely important by 57.9% of the respondents, is the critical incident scale. Critical requirements "include those which have been demonstrated to have made the difference between success and failure

Exhibit 13. Excerpt from a Weighted Check List

SUPERVISOR'S APPRAISAL OF EMPLOYEE'S JOB PERFORMANCE

NAME OF EMPLOYEE _____ DEPARTMENT _____

JOB TITLE _____ DATE OF APPRAISAL _____

QUALITY OF WORK	☐ Much of work just barely gets by. Work requires constant checking to eliminate mistakes he should recognize himself. Low standards as to neatness. 0 PTS	☐ Work requires checking due to some lack of care, interest or other reasons. Work not quite as neat as it should be. 1-5 PTS	☐ Most of work done well. Usually acceptable in both accuracy and neatness. 6-10 PTS	☐ Very few errors, usually minor in nature. Work seldom has to be done over. 11-15 PTS	☐ Mistakes extremely rare. Merits complete confidence in ability to do quality work without close supervision. If checking work of others, rarely fails to find existing errors. 16-20 PTS
QUANTITY OF WORK	☐ Seldom gets work done in required time. Slow. 0 PTS	☐ Output not always up to amount described in performance standard for this job. 1-5 PTS	☐ Turns out the normal amount of work but seldom more. 6-10 PTS	☐ Output exceeds amount described in the performance standard for this job. 11-15 PTS	☐ Volume of work is extraordinarily high. Usually does considerably more than expected of average person in job. 16-20 PTS
JOB KNOWLEDGE	☐ Leans heavily on others for procedures he should know. Slow learner. 0 PTS	☐ Has acceptable knowledge of most phases of job, but leans on others in some phases of job. 1-5 PTS	☐ Shows adequate personal knowledge of all parts of job. Can proceed without special instructions on all regular work. 6-10 PTS	☐ Has very good knowledge of all parts of job. Without special instructions can proceed correctly on many unusual matters (as well as routine) 11-15 PTS	☐ Has most exceptional knowledge of job and spends time studying other phases of dept. work. Others in job class look to him for correct procedures. 16-20 PTS
APPLICATION TO WORK	☐ Spends much time away from desk. Often interrupts work for idle talk. Usually tardy. Waits for assignments. 0 PTS	☐ Spends more time than necessary in talk or away from desk. Due to own poor planning is idle at some times but unable to handle volume at others. Often tardy. 1-3 PTS	☐ Spends no more time than necessary in talk or away from desk. Shows fair planning to keep busy. Sometimes tardy. 4-6 PTS	☐ Usually on the job at all times. Very little idle time. Industrious. Rarely tardy. Does a good day's work. 7-9 PTS	☐ Energetic. Loses no time in starting and works right to the last minute. Plans work in advance so as to avoid delays. Never tardy. 10-12 PTS

in carrying out an important part of the job assigned in a significant number of instances" (Flanagan, 1954, p. 329). Critical incidents are reports by knowledgeable observers of things employees did that were especially effective or ineffective in accomplishing part of their jobs. Critical incidents are recorded as they occur for each employee by his or her supervisor. They provide a behaviorally based starting point of extreme behaviors for appraising performance (Cascio, 1978; DuBrin, 1980).

The advantages of this technique are that ratees will receive meaningful feedback and that supervisors discuss real incidents with the employee. In addition, Flanagan and Burns (1955) suggested that when a large number of critical incidents are collected, abstracted, and categorized they can be applied to training programs, selecting and classifying employees, and designing of equipment.

As with other approaches of performance appraisal, the critical incident method has some disadvantages. The technique becomes time consuming and burdensome when supervisors record incidents for all of their subordinates on a daily basis or even weekly basis (Cascio, 1978; Haynes, 1978; Scott, 1973). Due to this time problem, feedback is often delayed.

Graphic Rating Scales

Another method based on the behavioral content domain is the rating scale. The graphic rating scale, introduced by Patterson in 1922, is the oldest quantitative performance appraisal technique. It was considered important by 57.2% of our respondents. In this method, the rater is supplied with a printed form for each employee to be rated. The form contains a number of job performance qualities and characteristics to be evaluated. The rater subjectively scores each item on a continuum from a low to a high degree of the factor being appraised. An example is presented in Exhibit 14.

Graphic rating scales vary in three respects: (1) the degree to which the meaning of the response category is defined; (2) the degree to which the individual who is interpreting the ratings (e.g. personnel manager) can tell clearly what response was intended; and (3) the degree to which the performance dimension being rated is defined for the rater (Cascio, 1978; Guion, 1965; Ivancevich et al., 1980; Landy and Farr, 1980).

Graphic rating scales may not yield the depth of narrative essays or critical incidents but they are less time consuming to administer,

Exhibit 14. Graphic Rating Scale Form

PERFORMANCE — Engineering Personnel Annual Appraisal

1. QUALITY OF WORK

UNSATISFACTORY	MARGINAL	ACCEPTABLE	COMMENDABLE	OUTSTANDING
Poor quality of work, continually makes errors, requires excessive checking and rework.	Careless, inclined to make mistakes, work barely acceptable.	Meets minimum requirements of accuracy and neatness, average quality of work, needs normal supervision.	Exceeds minimum requirements of accuracy and neatness, very few errors, carries out instructions well, needs little supervision.	Consistent high degree of accuracy and neatness, work can be relied upon, very little rework, seldom needs supervision.

REMARKS: _____

2. ATTENDANCE

UNSATISFACTORY	MARGINAL	ACCEPTABLE	COMMENDABLE	OUTSTANDING
Often absent or tardy. Does not report absence or tardiness in advance. Very Undependable.	Erratic in attendance and punctuality. Seldom reports absence or tardiness in advance. Not dependable.	Occasionally absent or tardy. Reports absence or tardiness in advance.	Seldom absent or tardy. Always reports absence or tardiness in advance. Dependable.	Excellent attendance record. Always at work and on time. Very dependable.

REMARKS: _____

3. JOB KNOWLEDGE

UNSATISFACTORY	MARGINAL	ACCEPTABLE	COMMENDABLE	OUTSTANDING
Definite lack of knowledge. Very little understanding of job duties. Needs considerable instructions.	Inadequate knowledge of duties. Understanding of job duties not sufficient.	Has adequate knowledge of duties. Needs a little additional instruction.	Good knowledge of duties. Well informed. Occasionally needs direction.	Excellent understanding of job assignments. Requires very little direction. Extremely capable.

REMARKS: _____

4. ATTITUDE

UNSATISFACTORY	MARGINAL	ACCEPTABLE	COMMENDABLE	OUTSTANDING
Difficult to work with. Chip-on shoulder attitude. Uncooperative. Rude.	Occasionally unwilling to follow orders without argument. Inclined to be stubborn.	Tries to cooperate. Usually agreeable and obliging.	Cooperative most of the time. Interested in work. Quick to offer assistance.	Always cooperative. Shows a high interest in work. Goes out of way to help. Pleasant.

REMARKS: _____

(Adapted from an exhibit in *How to Improve Performance Through Appraisal and Coaching,* by Donald L. Kirkpatrick. New York: AMACOM, 1982.)

permit quantitative results to be determined simply, are dimensionally heterogeneous, and can be used for comparisons among employees (Cascio, 1978).

Behaviorally Anchored Rating Scales

In 1963, Smith and Kendall introduced behavioral expectation scaling, which became alternatively known as the Behaviorally Anchored Rating Scale (BARS). The first step for the development of BARS is to ask persons with knowledge of a group of similar jobs (jobholders and/or supervisors) to describe specific incidents critical to performance. These incidents are then clustered into five or ten performance dimensions which are defined. A second group of persons, similarly familiar with the job set, is given the incidents and the definitions of performance dimensions; they are asked to assign each incident to the dimension it best fits (retranslation).

An incident is retained in the design if 50-80 percent of both groups agree upon its dimension assignment. This second group is asked to rate the behavior described in each incident as to whether it represents effective or ineffective behavior. The result is a rating scale that has examples of behavior to anchor each degree (Fogli, Hulin, & Blood, 1971; Schwab, Heneman & DeCottiis, 1975).

Examples of BARS items used in an appraisal can be seen in Exhibit 15.

The advantage of the behaviorally anchored rating scale is that it concentrates on the behavior of the employee, not his/her personality. However, the scale requires a great amount of time and effort to be successfully implemented. The scales must be continuously updated and validated to ensure that the behaviors specified are still relevant to the job.

The BARS technique is applicable for administrative and developmental purposes. Since the levels of performance are anchored, the appraiser can give feedback to the employee on which dimensions s/he is weak or strong.

Although there have been numerous articles in the past decade expounding the benefits of BARS, Exhibit 12 indicates that only 23% of our survey respondents reported it to be of moderate or greater importance in their performance appraisal processes. The broad majority (69.1%) state that it is not applicable in their companies.

OUTCOME-ORIENTED TECHNIQUES

Some appraisal methods concentrate their attention on the specific accomplishments or results achieved by the employee. Ex-

Exhibit 15. Example of a Behaviorally Anchored Rating Scale (BARS) Item

Job Dimension: Planning of Research Studies

7 [ ] EXCELLENT— Plans for flow of research studies several years ahead. Develops and implements project plans so that all research studies are produced on schedule and within budget for the reporting period. Maintains an acceptable number of studies in processes to assure meeting production schedule requirements. Knows the status of any project against milestones at all times.

6 [ ] VERY GOOD— Develops and implements research project plans with supporting timelines, so as to be able to determine the exact status of all projects at any given time. Ensures completion of projects on time and budget. Does not maintain a regular flow of new studies, leading to potential problems in the future.

5 [ ] GOOD— Monitors projects against existing milestones, trying to ensure research, analysis and report writing will be performed in a timely manner to allow for completion

amples are the direct index method, the standards-of-performance approach, and the management-by-objectives (MBO) approach.

Two forces have increased the interest in these outcome-oriented appraisal techniques in the past 25 years. One is that gains in productivity have been coming at a decreased rate. It has been pictured that a focus on results—a commitment to achieve specific goals, and a system providing rewards for reaching them—could help to turn the productivity curve upward again. Another force is the concern that qualitative, unspecific, subjective appraisal methods—especially those that assess traits of the individual—produce more heat than light in feedback interviews. This observation was convincingly pre-

> of required projects against time and budget constraints. Has some problem maintaining a continuous flow of new studies into the research cycle.
>
> 4 [ ] AVERAGE— Monitors research study projects, interacting with authors, data analysts and others to facilitate meeting time and budget constraints. Experiences some slippages in schedule due to unanticipated problems. Develops all milestones in an optimistic manner.
>
> 3 [ ] BELOW AVERAGE— Monitors mainly projects which need to be completed in the near future. Checks with researchers on other project progress only irregularly. Does not maintain a weekly schedule to ensure lack of study slippages against milestones. Does not report such slippages, resulting in scheduling problems.
>
> 2 [ ] VERY POOR— Does not plan ahead for research activities. Often fails to meet commitments for research outputs. Does not develop milestones against which study progress can be measured.
>
> 1 [ ] UNACCEPTABLE— Does not complete research studies as required or within budget. Manages by putting out fires as they erupt.

sented by Douglas McGregor in a landmark 1957 paper since underscored by many other authorities. A focus on specific work results and on factors that visibly affect results is seen as leading to more favorable motivation toward improvement.

The Direct Index

With this approach, individuals are evaluated solely on the basis of the results they have achieved. For each job, several appropriate measures of output or results are identified and combined to form a numerical index. As Meidan (1981) notes, for a marketing executive, the index used might include sales, turnover, market share, and profit. These would reflect the efficient use of sales personnel and of marketing variables such as price, promotion, product development and distribution.

The advantage of the direct index method is that it avoids errors of perception and biases on the part of the appraiser.

The disadvantage is that changes in the index number may not always represent changes in the employee's performance. The index may be influenced by the state of the business economy, the effective work of other employees, etc. Also, in a feedback session, little fact-based information can be given for developmental purposes.

Standards of Performance

The performance standards approach compares actual accomplishments with a much more detailed set of expectations. In place of an index number that provides a global goal, a set of standards of performance for a position sets down a list of conditions that will exist when a job is being done well (Rowland, 1970). For each major job segment, one or more standards statements is written to complete the sentence, "The job of [position title] is well done when ...." As far as possible the standards are expressed in quantitative terms. If a way cannot be found to put the standard in measurable terms, it is framed so that at least the presence or absence of a specified outcome or activity can be verified (Enell and Haas, 1960). Qualitative standards may be written to describe the outcome for an occasional job segment which does not lend itself to a quantitative or verifiable aiming point.

In the most recommended procedure (Appley, 1943; Miller, 1966; Rowland, 1970), the standards are arrived at through negotiation between the individual subordinate and superior, or between a group of subordinates (such as product managers) with the same responsibilities and their chief. The negotiation between superior and subordinates is neither "top down" nor "bottom up". It is an interchange of thinking, experience and data as to what needs to be achieved, what obstacles must be overcome, and what level of accomplishment is achievable. An example of a set of performance standards is given in Exhibit 16.

At the end of an appraisal period, the superior and subordinate meet to compare the subordinate's actual results with the agreed-on standards, recording those that the facts show to have been fully met, almost met, partly met, etc. The subordinate is encouraged to explain

Exhibit 16. Example of Standards of Performance for a Production Foreman

Significant Job Segments	*The job of the PRODUCTION FOREMAN is well done when:*
1. Safety	A. Monthly safety meetings are conducted in accordance with company schedules.
	B. Safe operating procedures are followed by all employees.
	C. Regular monthly inspections are held in the department in accordance with the approved checklist.
	D. Action is taken within five days to correct any unsafe condition.
	E. Monthly safety reports are submitted by the 5th of the month.
2. Controlling Costs	A. Waste and scrap are kept below 2% of total production.
	B. One cost saving improvement per month is developed and put into operation.
	C. Overtime costs are held to a maximum of 3% of direct labor costs.
	D. Overhead costs are kept within budget limitations.
	E. Salary controls are exercised in accordance with the salary administration plan.
	F. At least two team projects a year are undertaken to eliminate causes of significant scrap losses.
	G. The ratio of productivity to costs is improved by 1% every 6 months.
3. Developing Subordinates	A. New employees are inducted and trained in accordance with a definite plan.
	B. Performance reviews are held with all subordinates on at least an annual basis.
	C. Discussions are held with subordinates at least quarterly to see that performance improvement takes place according to plan.
	D. Responsibilities and authority are delegated to subordinates on a planned basis.

[Adapted from an exhibit in *How to Improve Performance Through Appraisal and Coaching*, by Donald L. Kirkpatrick. New York, AMACOM, 1982.]

how the variances came about, and to suggest how to overcome them. Also, at this interview, revised standards or additional standards for the next appraisal period may be agreed upon.

The advantages of the standards approach are:

- The participative approach gives both subordinate and superior a method of sharing thoughts about the priorities of the various job segments and about the results to be targeted.
- The cooperative standard setting tends to earn the subordinates's commitment to achieve the standards, and the superior's commitment to provide support and resources.
- The subordinate is not surprised by the appraisal results at the end of the period; the standards are known all along, so the subordinate can spot any variances as they develop and has a chance to correct them before the time of the appraisal.
- Appraisals and feedback interviews are more objective and less contentious because they are based on specified outcomes in the principal job segments rather than on personal attributes.

The principal disadvantage of the performance standards approach is the amount of time and thought required to talk out the job priorities and work up standards for all the significant segments of each job. It takes effort to come to agreement on performance standards and define them in clear and measurable terms. Though the time is not easy to find, it is well spent, standards users say. The process requires managers to identify, describe and weigh the various job objectives and results.

Exhibit 17 shows that fully 77.8% of the respondents report that performance standards/goals methods are either moderately important, very important or extremely important in their companies. More companies give high ratings to these methods than to any of the other methods scored in the survey.

Management by Objectives

Like performance standards, the goals in the management-by-objectives (MBO) approach are specific to each position. A set of MBO goal statements, however, focuses on perhaps six to ten key results that are to be achieved within the period between appraisals or by specific dates. MBO statements often specify milestones—or "specific deliverables" as Robert Schreiber of Salomon Brothers

Exhibit 17. Importance of Outcome-Oriented Methods As Perceived in Respondents' Companies

	Perf. Stds., Goals
Extremely important	40.5%
Very important	28.4
Moderately important	8.9
Slightly important	5.1
Not important	3.5
Not applicable in our company	13.6

termed them—rather than levels of effectiveness that will be acceptable on a continuing basis. Thus MBO objectives usually devote more attention than performance standards to *what is to be changed* in the coming period. An example of a set of MBO goals is shown in Exhibit 18.

Negotiation between subordinate and superior is widely recommended for MBO goal setting (Odiorne, 1965; Valentine, 1966; McConkey, 1976). Vincent Conte of the Insurance Services Office explained:

> Goal setting takes place at the start of any performance period. Ideally, the supervisor and the subordinate negotiate goals to the point at which they are in mutual agreement. We also encourage supervisors to record these goals and keep them in the individual's file to be referred to when the final evaluation is prepared.

Asked about his company's process for negotiating goals, Robert Schreiber of Salomon Brothers added:

> A "negotiating process" sounds very formal. I prefer to think of what we have as discussions. This really depends on how a manager likes to manage. I ask my people to write their performance plan and give it to me for review. I give them written feedback on it. They modify it if they want to, and then we meet to discuss areas that we agree and disagree on. We've had some cases where I felt they were overly optimistic, and I've even taken objectives off or scaled back the time frame in which one should be accomplished. In other cases, I didn't

> **Exhibit 18. Example of MBO Goals for a Sales Manager**
>
> Key results as detailed here will be attained during fiscal 198___.
>
> 1. Increase penetration (in share of market) in the Southeast Region for the _____ Division from ___% to ___% during 198___.
> 2. Open ___ branches in the Southeast Region before September 15.
> 3. Revise field sales reporting procedures during 198___ so consolidated reports can be issued ___ days earlier.
> 4. Establish by April 15 a procedure for handling and analyzing customer complaints.
> 5. Send a bulletin on minimum order size and trade discounts to the company's customer list for Product X by February 15.
> 6. During fiscal 198___, increase direct product profit for Product Family Z by ___% over the fiscal 198___ rate.
> 7. During August, conduct a series of regional meetings to review past results and introduce the marketing plans for Product M.
> 8. During fiscal 198___, reduce direct selling expense to ___% of net sales.
> 9. Issue by January 30 a new bulletin on collecting credit information on new accounts.
> 10. By July 30, investigate the potential net gain in sales volume and standard profit contribution that could be realized if hardware stores are added to present channels of distribution.
>
> [Synthesized from a number of specimens of MBO statements]

think they were aggressive or precise enough. It's a give and take activity.

At the end of the selected period, the appraiser observes the manager's actual results and compares them with the goals previously agreed on.

When MBO goals are set participatively, the advantages of the approach are similar to those just given for performance standards. In organizations and jobs undergoing rapid change, the emphasis on what is to be changed is a further advantage. Also, a set of MBO statements can be prepared more rapidly, since it mainly covers new accomplishments and new activities in selected segments of the job.

The principal disadvantage reported is that MBO's emphasis on a small number of specific milestones or accomplishments ignores a manager's effectiveness or ineffectiveness in other areas. The manager may win high credits for completing specified projects or reaching a sales goal, but meanwhile morale of the person's group may have plummeted due to poor personnel practices, or control of costs may have been lost.

As Dr. William H. Bleuel, partner in the management consulting firm of Zarkov and Gordon, Ltd., commented in an interview:

> In most companies, the MBO approach biases the appraisal toward the selected objectives, which frequently are short term. The performance appraisal may not allow for heavy weighting of the relationships that would have longer term benefits. For example, it does not consider team building on a continuing basis.

Provision needs to be made for monitoring these ongoing responsibilities as well as the immediate targets.

COMPARISON OF APPRAISAL TECHNIQUES

The literature compares these techniques for their ability to minimize rater biases. The major biases discussed in the research on performance appraisal are: leniency, central tendency, and halo. After a brief definition of each bias, a summary of the comparative research on these techniques will be presented.

Leniency errors occur when the rater assigns all employees high performance ratings and all scores cluster at top levels of the measurement instrument. Raters subscribe to their own set of assumptions (which may or may not be valid). Raters may be either inordinately easy (positively lenient) or inordinately difficult (negatively lenient).

Central tendency errors occur when raters avoid using the high and low extremes of rating scales and tend to cluster all ratings about the center of each scale. "Everybody is average" is one way of expressing the central tendency error.

The halo effect is perhaps the most pervasive error in performance appraisal. A rater who commits the halo error assigns ratings on the basis of a global impression of the ratee (Thorndike, 1920). A subordinate is rated either high or low on most items because the rater knows (or thinks he knows) that the subordinate is high or low on some specific factor. The rater fails to distinguish among the levels of performance on different performance dimensions. Ratings contaminated by the halo error show spuriously high positive intercorrelations and, therefore, fail to portray accurately an individual's relative performance on different dimensions (Cascio, 1978).

When subjective appraisal techniques requiring a high degree of inference on the part of the rater are used, these and other errors can occur and will affect, or bias, the "operational discriminability" (DeVries, Morrison, Schullman & Gerlach, 1980) of the appraisal system. Operational discriminability occurs when a measurement properly distinguishes employees by level of performance (Kane and Lawler, 1979). Discriminability is a characteristic of the appraisal system that allows for a distribution of employees according to level of performance. It involves the degree to which a measure distinguishes among individual employees in terms of performance (Wesley, 1979). To obtain discriminability, the inherent variance ("noise") in the appraisal system itself must be small in comparison to the variance in performance among employees.

It is the opinion of the researchers that discriminability between employees should not be casually assumed in performance appraisal. The assumption underlying the appraisal should not be the discrimination of level of performance across employees. It should be the comparison of an employee's performance against the standards of performance of key job elements necessary for the completion of the job. The purpose of the technique should be to measure this comparison.

Unfortunately, the literature in the field is consistent with the former comparative analysis, which compares employees' performance. Thus, we are plagued by researchers seeking the "best" technique to minimize rater errors; this, as pointed out above, is based on an unrealistic assumption.

Notwithstanding this criticism, an analysis of the literature yields the following three conclusions:

- Comparative methods (e.g. ranking, paired comparison, forced distribution) control for leniency, central tendency, and halo error (Cascio, 1978; Haynes, 1978).
- There is inconclusive evidence as to whether leniency, central tendency, and halo error are controlled when using absolute methods (e.g. essay, critical incidents, BARS) (Borman and Dunnette, 1975; Hom, DeNisi, Kinicki and Bannister, 1980).
- No research exists comparing outcome oriented measures for leniency, central tendency, and halo errors (DeVries et al., 1980).

The conclusions drawn from the literature should not be considered complete for one attempting to make an informed decision regarding the selection of an appraisal technique. The first conclusion suggests that for psychometric superiority, we should be using comparative methods. However, these methods actually have limited application in an organization. The second conclusion offers no conclusive results as to whether one technique minimizes these errors or not. The literature just presents both sides of the argument.

A comparison of the techniques in this manner does not seem useful to someone who uses them. A more beneficial comparison would be between the purposes of an appraisal and the appraisal technique. As mentioned previously, no one in the literature has answered the question: "which technique should be used for which of the three purposes?"

Purposes and Techniques

The relationship between the appraisal technique and the purpose of the evaluation is illustrated in Exhibit 19. The "X" indicates that a specific technique has the ability to be used for that specific purpose. A "-" indicates that the very nature of the technique limits its suitability for that specific purpose. An "Ⓧ" indicates that the technique has the potential to be used for that specific purpose, although other requirements must be met as well.

It is obvious from this exhibit that when an organization decides on the purpose(s) of the appraisal, it limits itself to certain techniques. Alternatively, when an organization decides on an appraisal technique, it is also deciding on the purpose for the appraisal.

Comparative methods, such as ranking, paired comparison and forced distribution can only be used for administrative purposes. These methods do not provide appraisers with enough information to enable them to give feedback to the employee. Based on the fact that feedback cannot be given, it is impossible to use these methods for legal justifications. Feedback is one of the legal requirements for an organization's performance appraisal process.

Critical incidents, graphic rating scales and behaviorally anchored rating scales (BARS) have the potential to be used for administrative, developmental, and justificatory purposes, whereas, the weighted checklist and forced choice scales are most appropriate for administrative purposes.

Performance standards is an outcome approach to appraisal and can be used for all three purposes. The direct index can only be used for administrative purposes. Though the literature suggests that one can surmise a lot of information from just one "number," it is still just an index of one outcome measure. All other conclusions about the employee's performance would be highly subjective on the part of the appraiser.

Hence, if the purpose of an organization's performance appraisal

Exhibit 19. Relationship Between Appraisal Technique and Purpose

	Purpose		
Techniques	Administrative	Developmental	Justificatory
Comparative			
Simple Ranking	X	—	—
Paired Comparison	X	—	—
Forced Distribution	X	—	—
Absolute			
Essay	X	X	—
Weighted Checklist	X	—	—
Forced Choice	X	—	—
Critical Incidents	X	X	Ⓧ
Graphic Rating Scale	X	X	Ⓧ
Behaviorally Anchored Ratings	X	X	Ⓧ
Outcome			
Direct Index	X	—	—
Performance Standards	X	X	Ⓧ
Management by Objectives	X	X	Ⓧ

Legend:
X = the technique has the ability to be used for that specific purpose
— = the nature of the technique limits its suitability for that specific purpose.
Ⓧ = the technique has the potential to be used for that specific purpose.

[Adapted from DeVries, Morrison and Shullman, 1980]

is administrative, any of the approaches will be possibilities; but if an organization wants to use an appraisal for developmental purposes, the technique must be carefully selected. This is also the case if the organization wants to use the appraisal for legal justification. This third purpose, legal justification, is becoming increasingly important, yet only 4 of the 11 techniques in the literature seem to have the potential to be used for this purpose.

THE FEEDBACK INTERVIEW

The final step in the performance appraisal process is the review of performance with the person whose work has been appraised. Regardless of how or how often job performance is measured, it is important for the appraiser to provide formal feedback to the appraisee. Without systematic, constructive feedback the person appraised will have difficulty in making the corrections necessary to improve performance, in matching his/her individual job performance expectations with those of the appraiser, and in assessing the progress that is being made toward career goals. Most organizations whose practices have been reported in recent management literature have some form of feedback process, usually between the immediate supervisor and the employee (Field and Holley, 1975; Hay Associates, 1975; Zawacki and Taylor, 1976).

Our respondents reported they too have provision for such feedback. Nearly all (98.9%) said they hold performance review interviews. As shown in Exhibit 20, the broad majority conduct these sessions once a year.

The majority (71.5%) conduct structured feedback sessions, while another 24.7% describe their feedback as "informal communication."

Exhibit 20. Frequency of Feedback Interviews

Frequency	Percentage of Respondents
Once a year	73.5%
Twice a year	17.3
More than twice a year	8.1

Exhibit 21. Who Supplies the Appraisal Feedback?

Interview Conducted by	Percentage of Respondents
Appraiser	92.8%
Personnel Department	5.9
An external source	1.3

Such reviews may be conducted by a variety of individuals and small groups. As indicated in Exhibit 21, the appraisee most commonly meets with one of the primary appraisers—usually his or her immediate supervisor.

The appraiser and the appraised individual address several matters in these sessions. In descending order of prevalence, our survey found these to be: past progress; overall performance; development and training; new performance goals; new performance standards; and salary information. And as Exhibit 22 indicates, 79% of our respondents have the subordinate sign the appraisal form at this time.

The subtleties of the performance review discussion did not lend themselves to exploration in our survey, but they are worthy of study. Needless to say, the preparation and interview approach of the appraiser are different for interviews oriented to compensation, coaching, development and training, etc. The books by Kellogg (1975), Johnson (1979) and Kirkpatrick (1982) offer helpful recommendations.

Exhibit 22. Actions Taken During Feedback Interview

Action Taken	Percentage of Respondents
Review past progress	97.3%
Discuss overall performance	96.9
Employee signs appraisal form	78.8
Discuss training & development	77.3
Establish new performance goals	71.5
Establish new performance standards	61.9
Discuss salary information	49.6

Exhibit 23. Positive Effects of Appraisal Process As Reported by Respondents at User Companies

Organizational Goal	NA	Level of Positive Effect			
		None	Slight	Moderate	Extreme
High productivity	2.4%	7.2%	31.7%	51.4%	7.2%
High morale	2.4	15.3	35.5	40.3	6.5
Efficiency	2.4	9.3	32.1	51.2	4.9
Good organizational leadership	2.8	9.7	29.6	44.5	13.4
Organizational growth	2.8	24.0	33.3	31.7	8.1
Profit maximization	2.8	20.7	32.5	36.2	7.7
Organizational stability	3.3	19.3	31.6	38.1	7.8

ARE PERFORMANCE APPRAISALS WORTHWHILE?

As we have seen, performance appraisal is a managerial responsibility and process that is widely prevalent in the work environment. It has impact on compensation, training and development, career paths, and the legal status of the human resources function. Yet for many managers the thought of performance appraisal brings to mind mixed images—feelings that it is "motivational" but "sensitive"; "vital," "touchy," "compelling," "crucial." Is the performance appraisal effort worth it all? Does it have a positive or a negative influence on key organizational goals? We asked our respondents to assess performance appraisal's effect on a series of company goals. Exhibit 23 summarizes their replies. They say it *does* have a positive effect. The most frequent evaluation is that performance appraisal has a "moderate" or greater effect, particularly on leadership, productivity, and efficiency. Its effects on morale, organizational stability, profits, and company growth are also rated as positive but less powerful.

Appendix

Performance Appraisal Checklist

	Yes	No
1. Is the performance appraisal system based on the measure of effective employee behavior?	___	___
2. Is the performance appraisal based on an accurate reflection of job performance? (The overall measure of job performance is fundamentally related to critical aspects of the job).	___	___
3. Is the performance appraisal system based on a thorough analysis of the job?	___	___
4. Is the performance appraisal system based on job analysis data pertaining to: a) knowledge and skills? b) specific rates or levels (standards) of performance?	___ ___	___ ___
5. Does the appraisal system meet the criteria of Title VII federal guidelines?	___	___
6. Has empirical data been collected to prove the validity of the method for the purpose for which it is being used?	___	___
7. Does the performance appraisal method differentially discriminate against a specific subgroup of the working population?	___	___
8. Are performance ratings all job related?	___	___
9. Were performance measures developed through job analysis?	___	___
10. Are raters able to observe the performance they are to rate?	___	___
11. Are ratings collected and scored under standardized circumstances?	___	___
12. Have the employees been advised of the critical requirements of their jobs?	___	___

13. Are performance appraisals conducted at least once a year? _____ _____
14. Are the employees evaluated solely on the extent to which they fulfill the critical requirements of the job? _____ _____
15. Are rewards tied directly to performance? _____ _____
16. Was the job analysis conducted at a time when the job was reasonably stable? _____ _____
17. Are criterion measures reliable? _____ _____
18. Does the appraisal instrument enable the appraiser to differentiate good from poor performers? _____ _____
19. Do appraisers:
    a) have a thorough knowledge of the job? _____ _____
    b) have ample opportunity to see the individual on the job? _____ _____
    c) have the expertise in interpretation of what is seen? _____ _____
20. Do appraisers have formal training in:
    a) the appraisal system? _____ _____
    b) the appraisal instrument? _____ _____
    c) the job of individuals being evaluated? _____ _____
21. Are raters trained to reduce rating errors? _____ _____
22. Do subordinates have a high degree of participation in the performance appraisal? _____ _____
23. Do subordinates participate in the setting of specific goals they are to achieve? _____ _____
24. Are subordinates "free" to discuss problems that may be hampering their current job performance? _____ _____
25. Do the supervisor and subordinate agree on a plan of action to be taken until the next review? _____ _____

References

Albemarle Paper Company v. Moody, 422 U.S. 405 (1975)

Anastasi, A. *Psychological testing*. New York: MacMillan, 1976.

Appley, L. A. Management the simple way. *Personnel*, 1943.

Beacham, S. Managing Compensation and performance appraisal under the age act. *Management Review*, January 1979, 51-54.

Bell, R. R. Evaluating subordinates: how subjective are you? *S.A.M. Advanced Management Journal*, 1979, 36-44.

Borman, W. C., & Dunnette, M. D. Behavior based versus trait oriented performance ratings: an empirical study. *Journal of Applied Psychology*, 1975, 60, 561-565.

Brinkerhoff, D. W., & Kanter, R. M. Appraising the performance of performance appraisal. *Sloan Management Review*, Spring 1980, 3-16.

Brito V. Zia Company, 478 F. 2d 1200 (1978).

Brumback, G. B. & Vincent, J. W. Jobs and appraisal of performance. *Personnel Administration*, September-October 1970, 26-30.

Bureau of National Affairs, Management performance appraisal programs. *Personnel Policies Forum No. 104*, 1974.

Cascio, W. F. *Applied psychology in personnel management*. Virginia: Reston, 1978.

Cummings, P. W. *Open management guides to successful practice*. New York: AMACOM, 1980.

DeCottiis, T. and Petit, A. The performance appraisal process: a model and some testable propositions. *Academy of Management Review*, 1978, 635-646.

DeVries, D. L., Morrison, A. M., Shullman, A. L., & Gerlach, M. L. *Performance appraisal on the line*. (Technical Report Number 16.) North Carolina: Center for Creative Leadership, December 1980.

DuBrin, A. J. *The practice of supervision achieving results through people*. Texas: Business Publications, 1980.

Dunham, R. B. Job evaluation: two instruments and sources of pay satisfaction. Paper presented at the annual American Psychological Association Convention, 1978.

Dunham, R. B., & Taylor, S. M. Standardized job analysis and evaluation: reliability, validity, and utility. Paper presented at the annual American Association Convention, 1980.

Dunnette, M. D., & Kirchner, W. K. A checklist for differentiating different kinds of sales jobs. *Personnel Psychology*, 1959, *12*, 421-429.

Enell, J. and Haas, G. *Setting standards for executive performance.* New York: American Management Association, 1960.

Equal Employment Opportunity Commission, Uniform guidelines on employee selection. *Federal Register,* 1978, *43,* 38290-38309.

Feild, H. and Holley, W. H. Performance appraisal—an analysis of state wide practices. *Public Personnel Management,* 1975, *4,* 145-150.

Feild, H. S. and Holley, W. H. The relationship of performance appraisal system characteristics to verdicts in selected employment discrimination cases. Unpublished paper, 1981.

Flanagan, J. C. The critical incident technique. *Psychological Bulletin,* 1954, *51,* 327-358.

Flanagan, J. C., & Burns, R. The employee performance record: a new appraisal and development tool, *Harvard Business Review,* 1955, *33,* 1-8.

Fleishman, E. A. On the relation between abilities, learning, and human performance. *American Psychologist,* 1972, *2,* 1017-1032.

Flippo, E. B. *Personnel management.* New York: McGraw-Hill, 1980.

Fogli, L., Hulin, C. L., & Blood, M. R. Development of first level behavioral job criteria. *Journal of Applied Psychology,* 1971, *55,* 3-8.

Ford, R. C., & Jennings, K. M. How to make performance appraisal more effective. *Personnel,* March-April 1977, 51-57.

Fournies, F. Why Management appraisal doesn't help develop managers. *Management Review,* January 1974, 19-24.

Fournies, F. & Associates, *Performance appraisal—design manual.* Bridgewater, NJ: F. Fornies & Assoc., 1983.

Ghiselli, E. E. and Brown, C. W. *Personnel and industrial psychology* (2nd ed.). New York: McGraw-Hill, 1955.

Ghorpage, J., & Atchison, T. J. The concept of job analysis: a review and some suggestions. *Public Personnel Management.* 1980, 134-144.

Griggs v. Duke Power Company, 401 U. S. 424 (1971).

Guilford, J. P. *Psychometric methods* (2nd ed.). New York: McGraw-Hill, 1954.

Guion, R. M. *Personnel testing.* New York: McGraw-Hill, 1965.

Hay Associates, *Survey of human resource practices.* New York: Hay Associates, 1975.

Haynes, M. G. Developing an appraisal program—part 1. *Personnel Journal,* 1978, 14-19.

Henderson, R. *Performance appraisal theory to practice.* Virginia: Reston, 1980.

Hom, P., DeNisi, A. S., Kinicki, A. J., & Bannister, B. D. Behaviorally anchored rating scales vs. summated rating scales. Paper presented at the annual American Psychological Association Convention, 1980.

Ivancevich, J. M., Donnelly, J. H., & Gibson, J. L. *Managing for performance.* Texas: Business Publications, 1980.

Johnson, R. G. *The appraisal interview guide.* New York: Amacom, 1979.

Kane, J. S., & Lawler, E. E., III. Performance appraisal effectiveness: its assessment and determinant. *Research in Organizational Behavior,* 1979, *1,* 425-478.

Kellogg, M. S., *What to do about performance appraisal.* New York: AMACOM, 1975.

Kirkpatrick, D. L., *How to improve performance through appraisal and coaching.* New York: AMACOM, 1982.

Kleiman, L. S., & Durham, R. L. Performance appraisal, promotion and the courts: a critical review. *Personnel Psychology,* 1981, *34,* 103-121.

Klinger, D. E. When the traditional job description is not enough. *Personnel Journal,* 1979, 243-248.

Landy, F. J. and Farr, J. L. Performance rating. *Psychological Bulletin,* 1980, *87,* 72-107.

Latham, G. P., Wexley, P., Increasing productivity through performance appraisal. Reading, MA: Addison Wesley, 1981.

Lazer, R. I. and Wikstrom, W. S. *Appraising managerial performance: current practices and future directions.* New York: The Conference Board, 1977.

Levine, E. L., Ash, R. A., & Bennett, H. N. Exploratory comparative study of four job analysis methods. *Journal of Applied Psychology,* 1980, *65*(5), 524-535.

Locher, A. H., & Teel, K. S. Performance appraisal—a survey of current practices, *Personnel Practices,* 1977, 245-247+.

Lubben, G. L., Thompson, D. E., & Klasson, C. R. Performance appraisal: the legal implications of Title VII. *Personnel,* 1980, 11-21.

Mahoney, T. A., Sorenson, W. W., Verdee, T. H., & Nash, A. R. Identification and prediction of managerial effectiveness. *Personnel Administration,* January-February 1963, *26,* 12-22.

McConkey, D. D. *How to manage by results.* New York: AMACOM, 1976.

McCormick, E. J. *Job analysis: methods and applications.* New York AMACOM, 1979.

McCormick, E. J., Jeanneret, P. R., & Mecham, R. C. A study of job characteristics and job dimensions as based on the Position Analysis Questionnaire (PAW). *Journal of Applied Psychology,* 1972, *56,* 347-368.

McGregor, D. An uneasy look at performance appraisal. *Harvard Business Review, 1957, 35,* 89-94.

McGregor, D. *Leadership and motivation.* W. G. Bennis and E. H. Schein (Eds.) Massachusetts: The Massachusetts Institute of Technology, 1966.

Meidan, A. *The appraisal of managerial performance* (AMA Management Briefing). New York: AMACOM, 1981.

Meyer, H. H., Kay, E., & French, J. R. P., Jr. Split roles in performance appraisal. *Harvard Business Review*, 1965, *43*(1), 123-129.

Miller, Ernest C., *Objectives and Standards: An Approach to Planning and Control.* New York: American Management Association, 1966.

Morano, R. A. Down with performance appraisal. *Supervisory Management*, 1974, 18-23.

Morsh, J. E. Job analysis in the U.S. Air Force. *Personnel Psychology*, 1964, *37*, 7-17.

Odiorne, George S., *Management by Objectives*, New York: Pitman, 1965.

Odom, J. V. *Performance appraisal:* legal aspects (Technical Report Number 3). North Carolina: Center for Creative Leadership, May 1977. Revised by K. J. Edwards, March 1979.

Patterson, D. The Scott Company graphic rating scale. *Journal of Personnel Research* (now called Personnel Journal). 1922-1923, *1*, 361-376.

Plumlee, L. B., Machemehl, A. E. and R. F. Utter, *Improving Performance Evaluation—A Content Validation Guide.* New York: AMACOM, 1983.

Prien, E. P. and Ronan, W. W. Job analysis: a review of research and findings. *Personnel Psychology*, 1971, *24*, 371-396.

Raia, A. P. *Management by objectives.* Illinois: Scott, Foresman, and Company, 1974.

Ralph, P. M. Performance evaluation: one more try. *Public Personnel Management Journal*, 1980, 145-154.

Rowland, V. K. *Evaluating and improving managerial performance.* New York: McGraw-Hill, 1970.

Sanders, M. S., & Peay, J. M. *Employee performance evaluation and review: a summary of the literature.* Naval Ammunition Depot Technical Report, August 1974. (RDTR No. 282)

Schneier, D. B. The impact of EEO legislation on performance appraisals. *Personnel*, July-August 1978, *55*(4), 24-34.

Schwab, D. P., Heneman, H. G., III, & DeCottiis, T. A. Behaviorally anchored rating scales: a review of the literature. *Personnel Psychology*, 1975, *28*, 549-562.

Siegel, J. *Personnel testing under EEO.* New York: AMACOM, 1980.

Sloan, S., & Johnson, A. New context of personnel appraisal. *Harvard Business Review*, November-December 1968, 14-30+.

Smith, P. C., & Kendall, L. M. Retranslation of expectations: an approach to the construction of unambiquous anchors for rating scales. *Journal of Applied Psychology*, 1963, *47*, 149-155.

Uniform Guidelines on Employee Relation Procedures. *Federal Register*, 1978, *43*, no. 166.

Valentine, Raymond F., *Performance objectives for managers.* New York: AMACOM, 1966.

Wade v. Mississippi Cooperative Extension Service. 528 F.2d 508 (1976).

Zavala, A. *Military standard on task analysis.* U.S. Army Armamant R & D Command CM4 Ballistics Procurement Division, 1980.

Zawacki, R. A., & Taylor, R. L. A view of performance appraisal from organizations using it. *Personnel Journal*, 1976, 290-292+.